5-Minute Ocean Stories

WRITTEN BY

Gabby Dawnay

ILLUSTRATED BY

Mona K

MAGIC CAT PUBLISHING

NEW YORK

In this book, you'll find 5-minute
nature stories to read aloud.

Each one is a wonder of the deep blue sea . . .
waiting to be discovered by you!

At the end of each story, explore an informative
"ALL ABOUT" page with a grown-up.

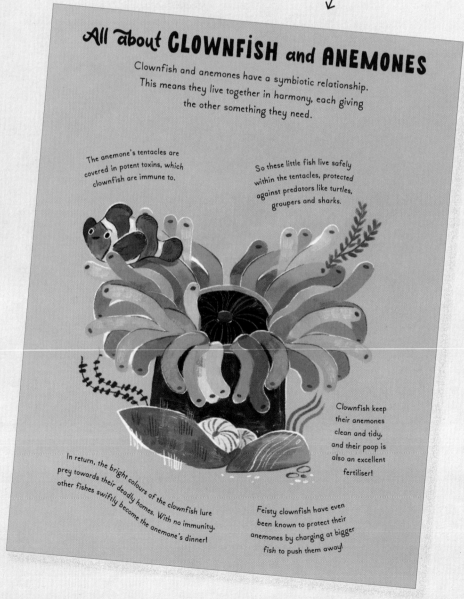

All about CLOWNFISH and ANEMONES

Clownfish and anemones have a symbiotic relationship.
This means they live together in harmony, each giving
the other something they need.

The anemone's tentacles are
covered in potent toxins, which
clownfish are immune to.

So these little fish live safely
within the tentacles, protected
against predators like turtles,
groupers and sharks.

Clownfish keep
their anemones
clean and tidy,
and their poop is
also an excellent
fertiliser!

In return, the bright colours of the clownfish lure
prey towards their deadly homes. With no immunity,
other fishes swiftly become the anemone's dinner!

Feisty clownfish have even
been known to protect their
anemones by charging at bigger
fish to push them away!

Which 5-minute OCEAN STORY will you read today?

The CLOWNFISH, the ANEMONE, and the BIG CORAL REEF

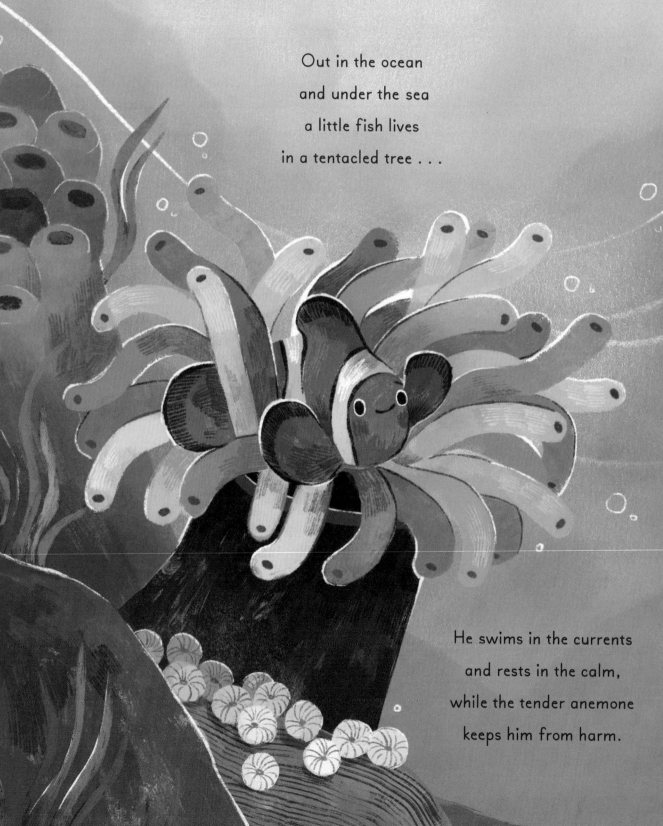

Out in the ocean
and under the sea
a little fish lives
in a tentacled tree . . .

He swims in the currents
and rests in the calm,
while the tender anemone
keeps him from harm.

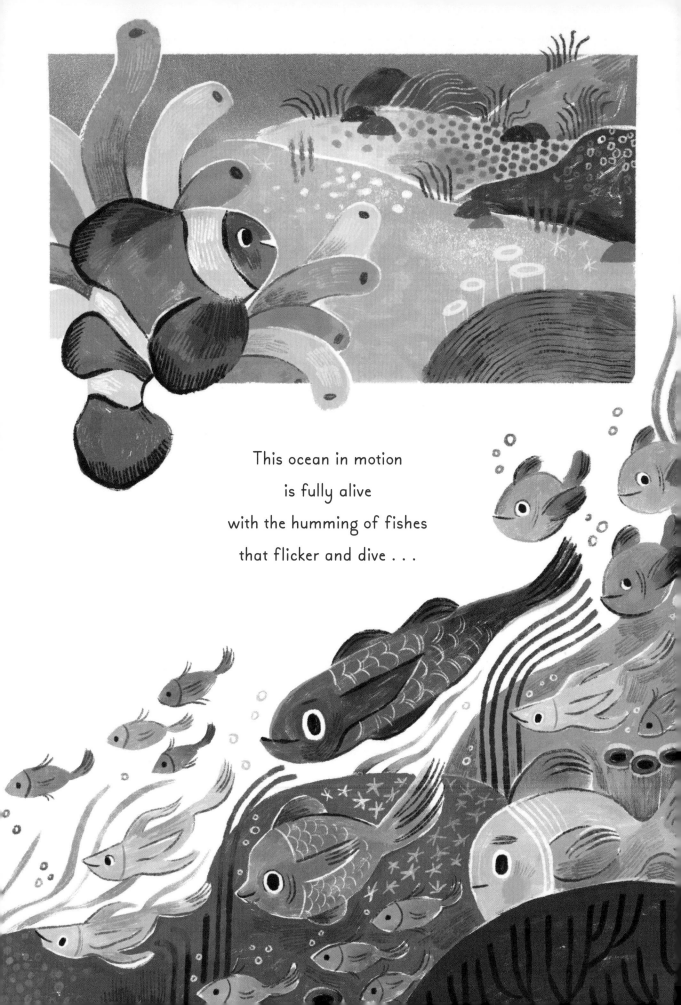

This ocean in motion
is fully alive
with the humming of fishes
that flicker and dive . . .

In a reef like a rainbow
of tapestry, spread
in a patchwork of patterns
across the seabed . . .

The water is clear and
the life here is teeming.
Content in his home,
little clownfish is dreaming . . .

*"Today I will leave,
for it's time to explore
every coral and crevice
from shipwreck to shore!"*

"I wonder what wonders await . . ." he begins
as he dashes away with a flick of his fins.

Past seahorses, sponges,
a lobster and clam,
he swishes his way
through the sea-traffic jam.

"My wonderful city is ever so busy,
but all of this traffic is making me dizzy!"

Then a hammerhead shark
with a dangerous grin
whispers, *"Come, little fish,
it is cozy within . . ."*

"Oh no!" gulps the clownfish,
and tries to keep steady,
*"I need to go home,
for my supper is ready!"*

Next from the shadows
emerges a grouper.
"Delicious!" he says,
"Are you supper? How super!"

The clownfish replies, *"I am terribly small,*
I am hardly a meal—I'm a mouthful, that's all!"

With a flicketty-skip he is off and away
and then, *"Sorry!"* he hollers. *"No supper today!"*

He dashes through seaweed
and splattering foam.
He has almost arrived
at his tentacled home . . .

When . . .

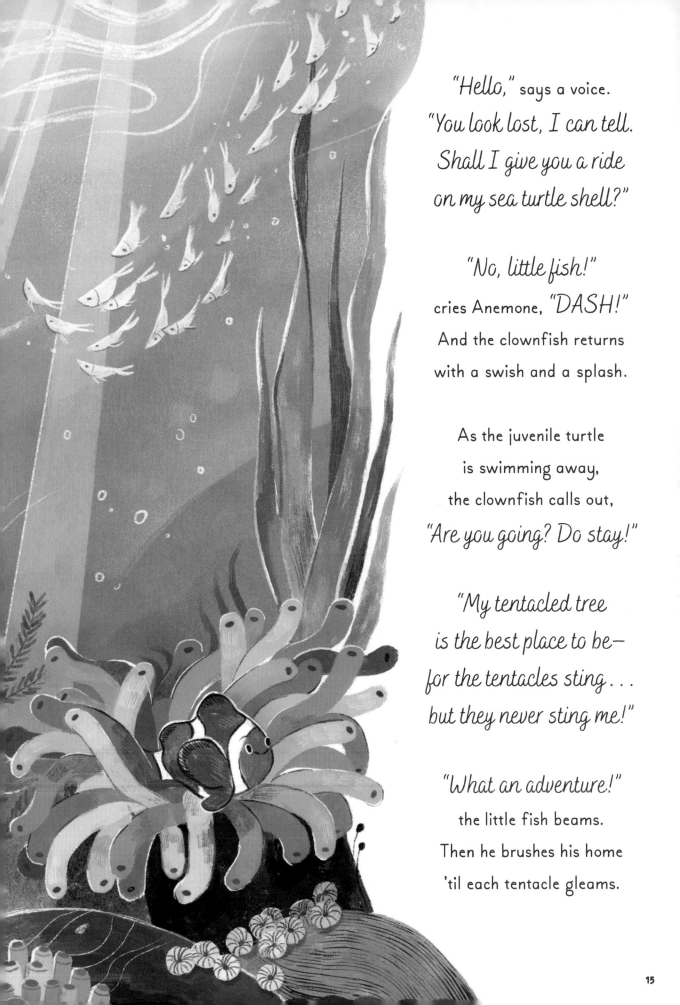

"Hello," says a voice.
"You look lost, I can tell.
Shall I give you a ride
on my sea turtle shell?"

"No, little fish!"
cries Anemone, "DASH!"
And the clownfish returns
with a swish and a splash.

As the juvenile turtle
is swimming away,
the clownfish calls out,
"Are you going? Do stay!"

"My tentacled tree
is the best place to be—
for the tentacles sting . . .
but they never sting me!"

"What an adventure!"
the little fish beams.
Then he brushes his home
'til each tentacle gleams.

All about CLOWNFISH and ANEMONES

Clownfish and anemones have a symbiotic relationship. This means they live together in harmony, each giving the other something they need. A clownfish rarely ventures far from its anemone.

The anemone's tentacles are covered in potent toxins, which clownfish are immune to.

So these little fish live safely within the tentacles, protected against predators, like groupers and sharks.

Clownfish keep their anemones clean and tidy, and their poop is also an excellent fertilizer!

In return, the bright colors of the clownfish lure prey toward their deadly homes. With no immunity, other fishes swiftly become the anemone's dinner!

Feisty clownfish have even been known to protect their anemones by charging at bigger creatures to push them away!

The water is waiting—
it's time to explore
every coral and crevice
from ocean to shore . . .

The GREAT WHITE SHARK'S
Tooth Machine

In cool coastal waters
a long way away,
a creature is cruising
around by the bay . . .

As quick as a trick,
she's a carnivore queen—
a magnificent fish
like a massive machine!

A bullet-shaped body
that's built to move fast,
see the smooth operator
accelerate past!

"I'm a fish with a swish and I cut quite a dash
as I sweep through the deep, racing past in a flash..."

"I am slick as a super-car—
what a design!
I am queen of the ocean—
the ocean is MINE..."

So silent and deadly, she slips through the waves,
sending multiple fishes to watery graves . . .

She glides like a vision
of flickering night,
with a smile that reveals
lots of sparkling white . . .

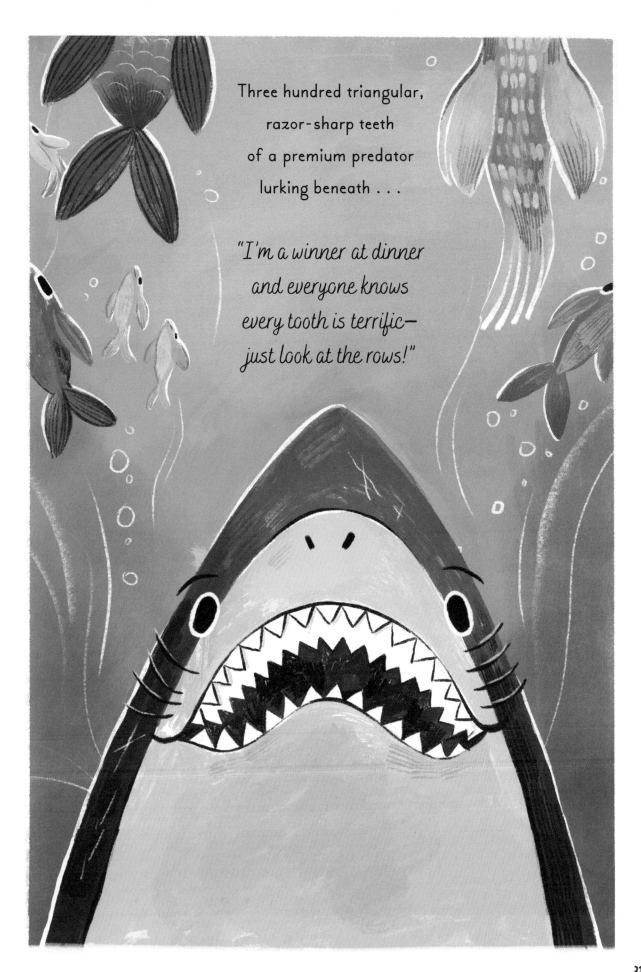

Three hundred triangular,
razor-sharp teeth
of a premium predator
lurking beneath . . .

*"I'm a winner at dinner
and everyone knows
every tooth is terrific—
just look at the rows!"*

"My mouth likes to munch
breakfast, dinner, and lunch,
and a fillet of fish in between . . .
But whatever your theory
I'm really not scary—
I much prefer ocean cuisine!"

Jaws full of triangles, sharp as a knife,
her teeth keep on growing throughout her whole life . . .

"I lose lots of teeth
when I bite on a snack,
so my new ones are ready
to quickly grow back!"

"My fixtures are flexible,
that is the aim—
see, my gnashers are set
in a cartilage frame . . ."

"For I am a hunter,
and terribly clever—
I need lots of teeth
so I'll grow them forever!"

"A constant supply—
a conveyor-belt feed
that will keep my mouth full
of the teeth that I need!"

A shark
with a smile
full of sparkling white . . .

. . . who glides like a vision
of flickering night!

Now look on the floor
of the ocean beneath . . .
see those gravestones galore?
They're gazillions of teeth!

All about the GREAT WHITE SHARK'S Tooth Machine

The magnificent, muscular great white shark is an apex predator and alpha carnivore—and its jaws are among the *most powerful* of any shark species.

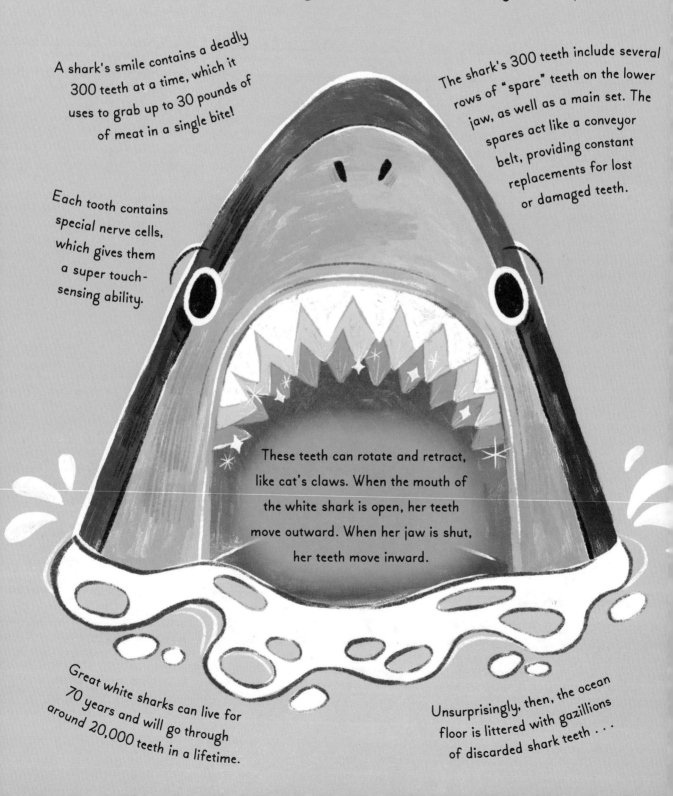

A shark's smile contains a deadly 300 teeth at a time, which it uses to grab up to 30 pounds of meat in a single bite!

The shark's 300 teeth include several rows of "spare" teeth on the lower jaw, as well as a main set. The spares act like a conveyor belt, providing constant replacements for lost or damaged teeth.

Each tooth contains special nerve cells, which gives them a super touch-sensing ability.

These teeth can rotate and retract, like cat's claws. When the mouth of the white shark is open, her teeth move outward. When her jaw is shut, her teeth move inward.

Great white sharks can live for 70 years and will go through around 20,000 teeth in a lifetime.

Unsurprisingly, then, the ocean floor is littered with gazillions of discarded shark teeth . . .

Someone is singing
a strange, lonely tale—
shall we swim for a while with the
song of the whale?

The SONG of the HUMPBACK WHALE

Down in the ocean
and deeper below,
a humpback is gliding
along with the flow . . .

Solo he journeys
alone through the sea.
Oh the whale is as lonely
as lonely can be . . .

All over the world
he is famous, renowned,
for his infrasound songs
singing, *"Hey, I'm around!"*

Finding his way between
water and ground,
his song makes a map
in a landscape of sound . . .

The notes travel quickly,
repeating and changing–
a musical movement
of data exchanging . . .

"Unbroken, unending,
the songs I am sending
revolve through the seas
and evolve 'til they're trending!"

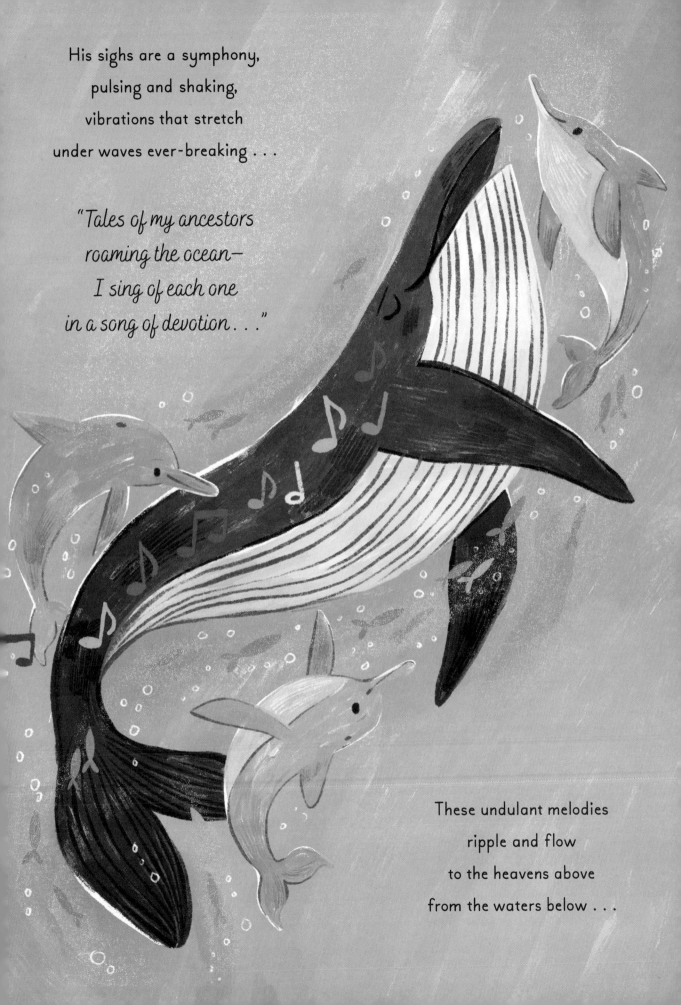

His sighs are a symphony,
pulsing and shaking,
vibrations that stretch
under waves ever-breaking . . .

"Tales of my ancestors
roaming the ocean—
I sing of each one
in a song of devotion . . ."

These undulant melodies
ripple and flow
to the heavens above
from the waters below . . .

"I sing of my journey, I sing of the deep.
Every moment of song is a memory I keep . . ."

An island in motion through oceans so vast,

where the future is always in tune with the past . . .

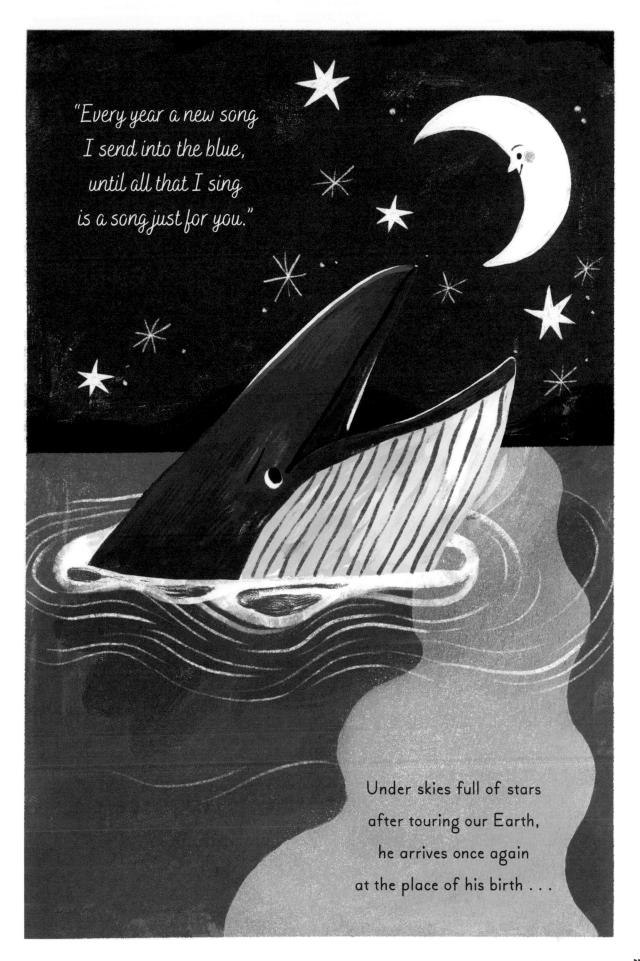

"Every year a new song
I send into the blue,
until all that I sing
is a song just for you."

Under skies full of stars
after touring our Earth,
he arrives once again
at the place of his birth . . .

*"My journey is lonely—
I'm longing to find
that special companion
who's one of a kind . . ."*

And the humpback,
so beautifully blacker than blue,
carries on with his song,
singing *"Love, love me do . . ."*

But wait! There's a shimmer . . .
a shadow moves past.
Could it be?
It is she!
He has found her—at last!

All about the HUMPBACK WHALE'S SONG

Humpback whales sing extraordinarily complex songs that can last for hours. Around 30 million years ago, whales evolved these long, low songs to communicate in the darkest depths of the ocean.

Sound travels four times faster underwater than it does through air. These songs of longing can stretch across the horizon into distant oceans.

Their songs are made up of many different noises, forming patterns and sequences, repeating harmonies that make each song unique.

Although both males and females make sounds, it's only the males who sing.
They sing songs to share information between humpback populations . . .
Songs to map and track their underwater world in landscapes of sound . . .
Songs to build relationships in the darkness.

Every year, whales migrate across the seas to the place of their birth, singing as they go.

And in the vastness of the ocean, they need to make a big noise.

As only males do the singing, it's thought they must be trying to find a mate.

Not starting or stopping—
our journey is bending
and folding through moments
of time never-ending . . .

The TIME-TRAVELING IMMORTAL JELLYFISH

The size of a fingernail—
barely a glimmer—
the time-bending jelly
glides by in a shimmer . . .

In tropical waters
surrounding the coast,
she floats through the waves
like a miniature ghost . . .

"My story is long—
it is more than one life,
moving forward and backward
through pleasure and strife..."

"Exploring the oceans
with every breath,
I am endless—eternal,
I often cheat death..."

"My name is Immortal—
I'm tiny and squishy.
My body is wobbly
and quite jelly-fishy!"

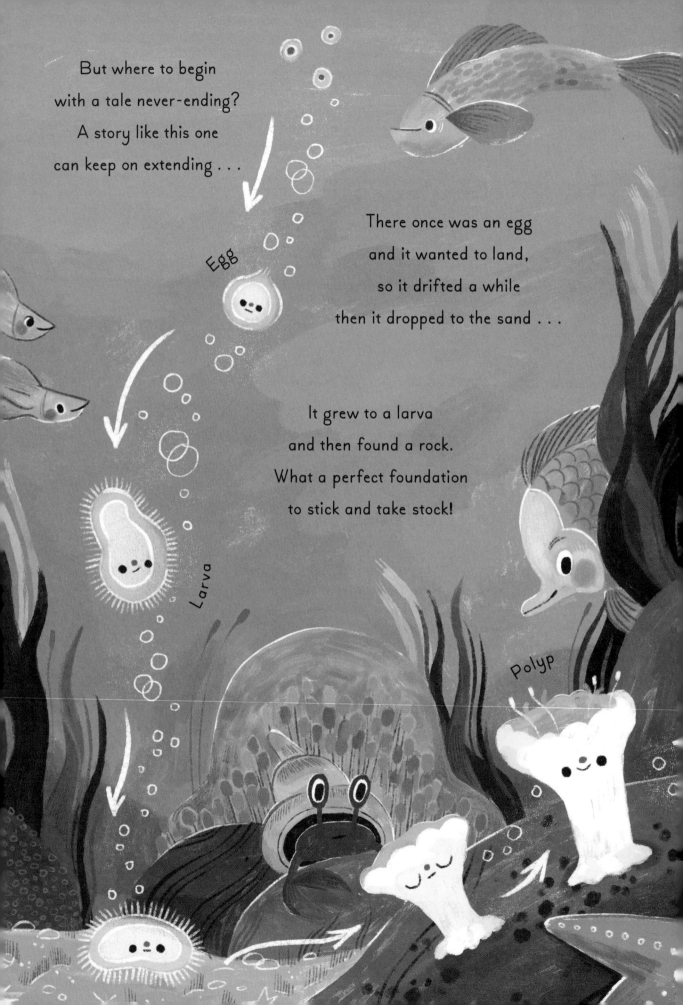

But where to begin
with a tale never-ending?
A story like this one
can keep on extending . . .

Egg

There once was an egg
and it wanted to land,
so it drifted a while
then it dropped to the sand . . .

It grew to a larva
and then found a rock.
What a perfect foundation
to stick and take stock!

Larva

Polyp

From larva to polyp,
it didn't stop growing,
until like a tree
tiny branches were showing . . .

Medusa!

The branches grew buds
and the buds broke away.
It was juvenile now
and it wanted to play . . .

Ephyra (juvenile)

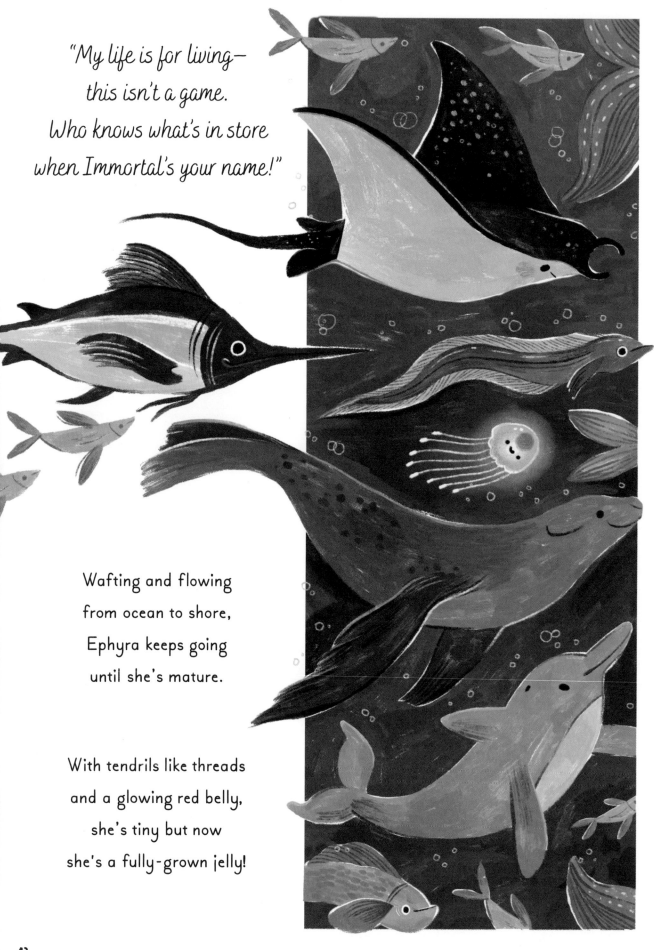

"My life is for living—
this isn't a game.
Who knows what's in store
when Immortal's your name!"

Wafting and flowing
from ocean to shore,
Ephyra keeps going
until she's mature.

With tendrils like threads
and a glowing red belly,
she's tiny but now
she's a fully-grown jelly!

But WAIT—there's no food.
Then the water goes COLD . . .
*"I am lost—I am shrinking.
I'll never get old!"*

As the jellyfish falls
to her soft sandy bed,
she begins to get younger
and younger instead . . .

Her tendrils retract
and her body gets small,
until—oh, she is barely
a jelly at all . . .

From cyst back to polyp,
her life will transform.
(With reverse metamorphosis,
this is the norm . . .)

*"A gateway through time is the way of immortals,
but we tiny jellies don't need to use portals . . ."*

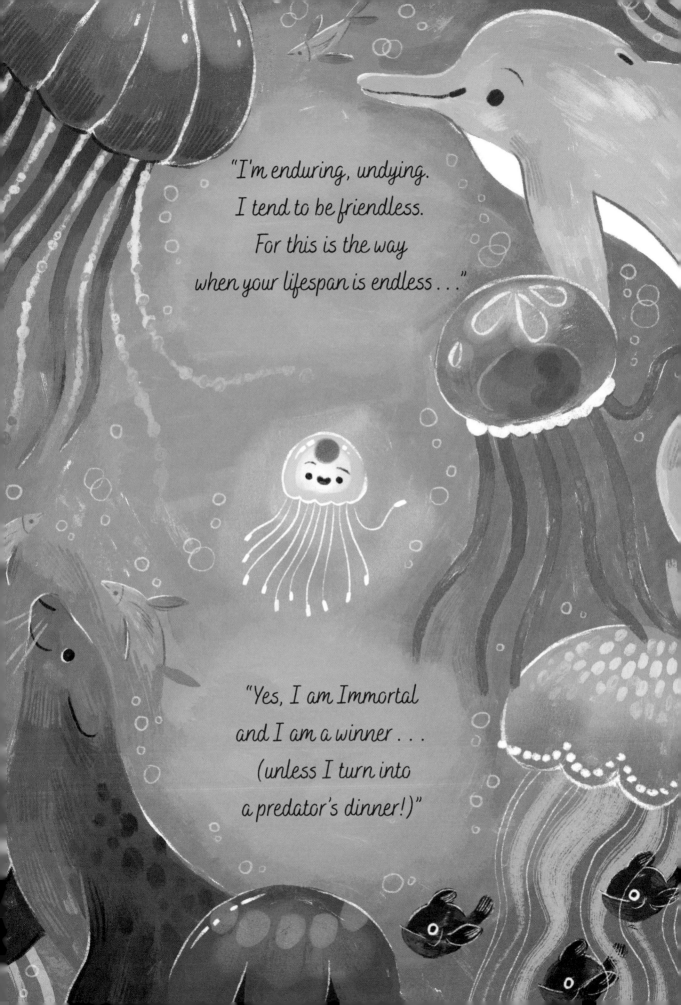

"I'm enduring, undying.
I tend to be friendless.
For this is the way
when your lifespan is endless . . ."

"Yes, I am Immortal
and I am a winner . . .
(unless I turn into
a predator's dinner!)"

All about IMMORTAL JELLYFISH

The immortal jellyfish (*T. dohrnii*) is quite possibly Earth's longest-living creature—
or at least, has the ability to be. Because this tiny animal can turn back
time using something called REVERSE METAMORPHOSIS.

1. A minuscule egg hatches into a larva, called a planula.

2. The larva, or planula, attaches itself to a rock or hard surface.

Reverse metamorphosis happens
if a medusa is injured, starved, or
drifts into waters too hot or too cold.
They drop to the seabed and transform
into a ball of tissue called a cyst.
This grows into a polyp again and so
the jellyfish continues its lifecycle.

3. There it turns into a polyp and grows little branches.

5. All being well, these grow into mature medusas. Females will lay eggs and males will fertilize them.

4. Buds break off the polyp, each becoming a juvenile called ephyra.

Like fluttering ribbons with curious features,
who knows where they go, these mysterious creatures?

The MIGRATION of the MAGICAL EEL

Our story begins
at the place it will end,
when a shimmer of swimmers
begins to descend . . .

Every one is a strange
and mysterious fish:
every one is an eel
that has swum with one wish . . .

To return to this ocean
of indigo blue,
just in time for
a marvelous eel rendezvous!

Every eel has arrived for one reason: to breed
in the orangey bloom of the Sargassum weed.

A massive migration
all coming to spawn.
Now from millions of eggs,
many millions are born!

So the babies are off!
On the current they float
through the ebb and the flow,
every one like a boat.

As soon as they hatch
with a sigh of relief,
every one of them looks
like a miniature leaf . . .

The larvae declare,
*"We would so love to stay
but there's no time to lose—
we must be on our way!"*

Their journey continues—
who knows what's in store
or the dangers they'll meet
before reaching the shore . . .

And something is happening . . .
See? As they pass,
every eel has become
as transparent as glass . . .

Tiny spaghetti strands
swimming with skill,
on and on they keep swimming
and swimming until . . .

They turn into elvers
that wriggle and swerve
with the flick of a snake
in a serpentine curve . . .

As slender as willows,
they ripple and fly
into rivers and streams
under watery sky . . .

So upstream they surge
like a flutter of tape,
each eel is emerging
in freshwater shape . . .

"These are my rivers
and here I belong.
I will stay and keep swimming
until I grow strong!"

Cylindrical body
all silky with slime,
the eel can grow up
to three feet over time.

From yellow to silver
with slip-slimy skin
made for riding and gliding
and slip-sliding in!

For years and for years
in the rivers they stay,
'til the moment arrives
and the eels must away . . .

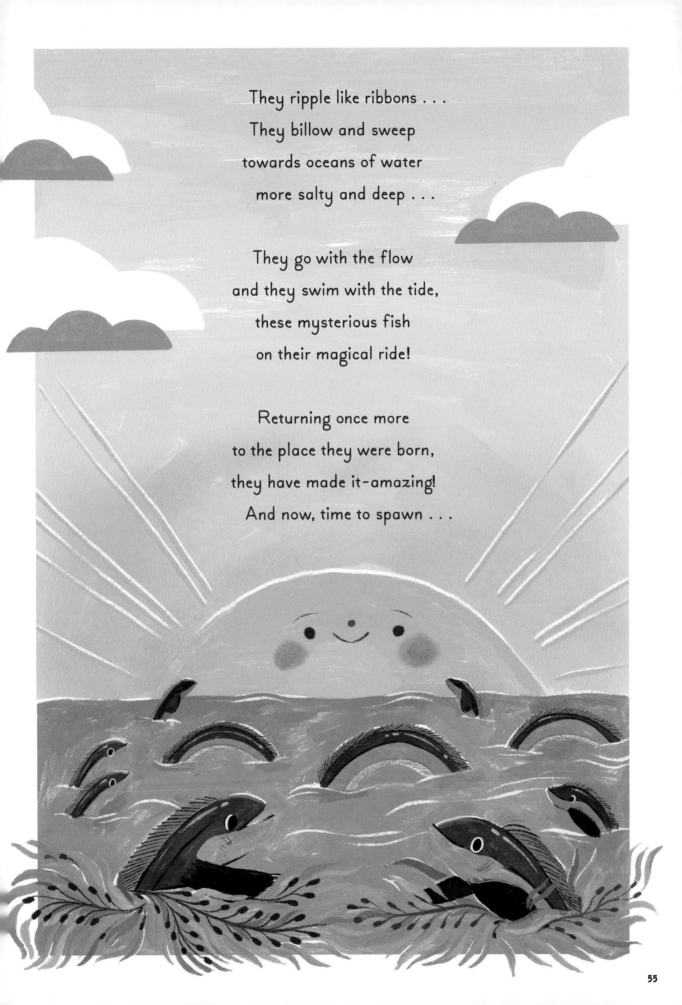

They ripple like ribbons . . .
They billow and sweep
towards oceans of water
more salty and deep . . .

They go with the flow
and they swim with the tide,
these mysterious fish
on their magical ride!

Returning once more
to the place they were born,
they have made it—amazing!
And now, time to spawn . . .

All about the MAGICAL EEL'S Epic Migration

Mature American eels return to the Sargasso Sea in the North Atlantic Ocean to spawn, the same place they were born years before . . .

1. Millions of minuscule eel eggs are carried along on warm currents.

2. They hatch and the tiny, leaf-like eel larvae continue on their epic journey that can span over 2,000 miles!

3. As they approach North America's east coast, they change into an eel-like shape. Now they look like transparent spaghetti!

Mysterious, snake-like, and sometimes alarming, the eel is disarming but ever so charming . . .

6. After many more years of swimming and eating, the eels reach maturity. These are silver eels and when the time is right, they ready themselves to return to the wide Sargasso Sea.

5. The juniors mature and their skin changes again. They are now yellow eels.

4. On arriving in freshwater rivers, the eels' skins darken and they become elvers.

Here is a forest. Let's wander inside
to the world of a cephalopod—
where does she hide?

The SHAPE-SHIFTING OCTOPUS

You'll find her in filigree
shadows that sway,
where the cuttlefish scoot
and the pufferfish play . . .

Sensational, sensitive,
super at healing:
Her body is soft. It's a body for feeling!

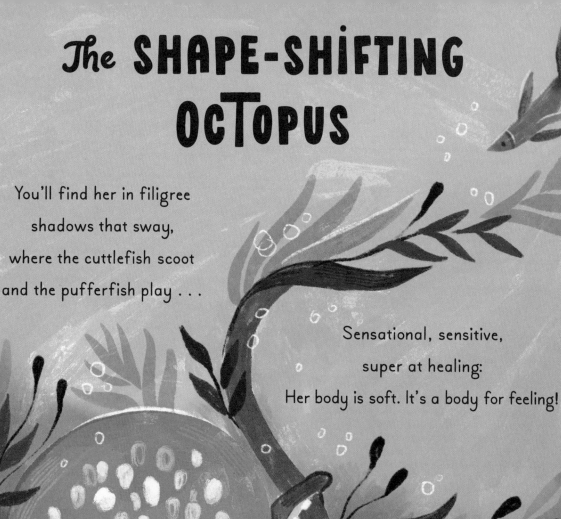

A shape-shifting drifter
though whispering night,
she has skin like a screen
made of shadows and light . . .

"Here is my home
in this garden of green.
It's the loveliest garden
you ever have seen!"

"Slippy and supple,
the wonderful weeds
form a sheltering wood
holding all that I need..."

The octopus moves
like a parachute blowing-
ballooning and billowing,
where is she going?

Swooping round coral
and over some shells
with a glittering shimmer
of silvery bells.

Her skin becomes textured,
her body transforms–
what magical camouflage tricks she performs!

And here she will wait for some good things to eat.
Maybe clams or a lobster-her favorite treat!

But what was that flickering-is she alone?
Or is somebody hiding behind the large stone . . . ?

OUT sweeps a shark from a gap in the rock
and he smiles: "Oh, hello . . . did I give you a shock?"

"YES!" cries the octopus,
waving her arms
as she scoots through the shoots
and away from his charms.

Quickly she flies, crying,
"Help me . . . oh HELP!"
as she weaves through
the forest of towering kelp.

Wafting and zooming
'round foliage blooming,
the octopus races,
her predator looming . . .

No bones in her body,
no bones in her head,
but brains-she has many!
"I'll use those instead . . ."

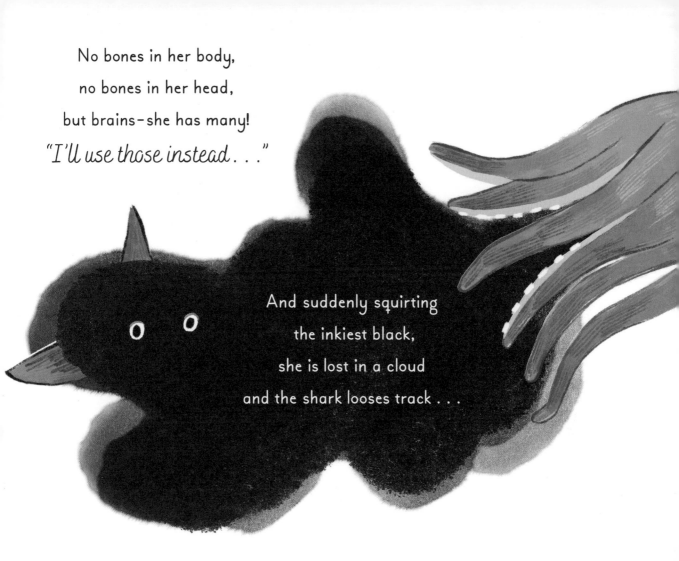

And suddenly squirting
the inkiest black,
she is lost in a cloud
and the shark looses track . . .

She races ahead through the emerald flow

while the shark lags behind thinking, *"Where did she go?!"*

With a flash then a glimmer,
the water is clear.
"So long!" She is gone
and will soon disappear . . .

Then spotting a gap
in the crack of a rock,
she maneuvers inside,
where she stops to take stock.

*"No bones in my body,
no bones make me free . . .
But brains, I have many—
I'm clever, you see!"*

*"Sensational, sensitive,
super at healing:
My body is soft.
It's a body for feeling!"*

A shape-shifting drifter
through whispering night,
she has skin like a screen
made of shadows and light.

All about the SHAPE-SHIFTING OCTOPUS

Octopuses have one of the best shape-shifting camouflage abilities in the world. They are seriously clever, having not one but NINE brains—one big "main" brain, plus a mini-brain in each of their eight arms.

Every arm can touch, taste, and move independently. And special sensors in their suckers mean they never get tangled up!

An octopus's brain-to-body ratio is the biggest of any invertebrate. They are terrific at solving puzzles and performing tasks. They can even use tools to build homes!

Having a soft, flexible, and entirely boneless body means that they have complete flexibility. Extending, bending, contracting, and flexing in any direction . . . the possibilities are endless!

A boneless body means they can squeeze into tiny nooks, crannies, and spaces. They can even regrow lost limbs!

The ocean is stormy—
a north wind is blowing.
Antarctica beckons,
and that's where we're going!

A PENGUIN'S SQUEEZE
in the FREEZE

Two emperor penguins
were happy to meet
in the icy Antarctic
all covered in sleet . . .

There weren't many places
the penguins could go,
so they swam in the ocean
and skated on snow.

A beautiful egg
made their family complete.
And then Ma said to Pa,
"Keep it warm on your feet!"

"Farewell now!" she whistled,
*"I know it seems rude
but I need to get going
to find us some food . . ."*

*"I won't be too long,
just be strong—and goodbye!"*
She said, *"Keep our egg cozy . . ."*
Said Papa, *"I'll try!"*

She slid on her tummy
and dives in the brine,
*"In a couple of months,
I'll be back—you'll be fine!"*

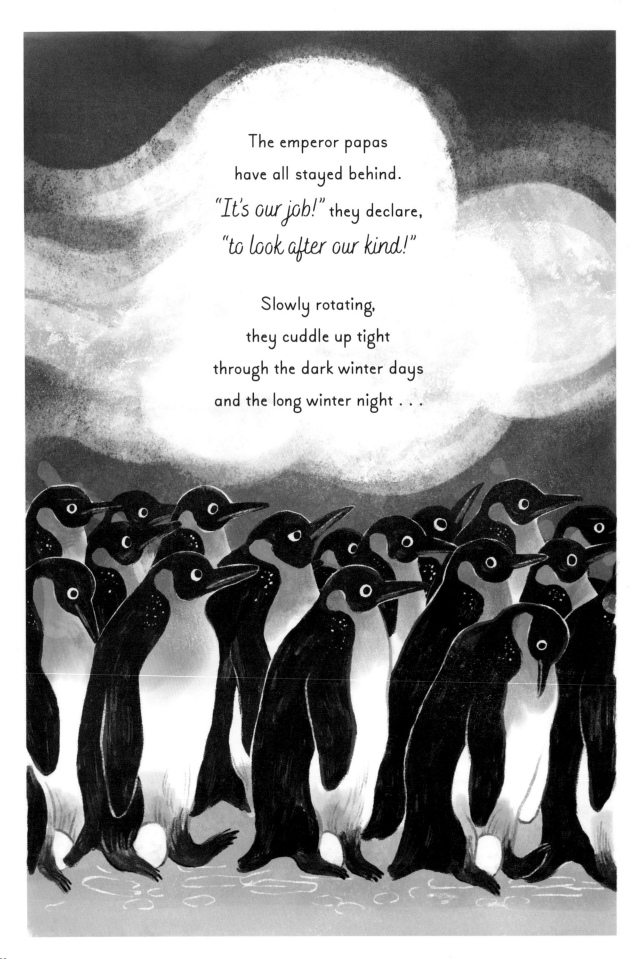

The emperor papas
have all stayed behind.
"It's our job!" they declare,
"to look after our kind!"

Slowly rotating,
they cuddle up tight
through the dark winter days
and the long winter night . . .

After 65 days . . .

every egg in its pouch
is beginning to hatch . . .

with a crack then an
OUCH!

It's chilly outside,
but no matter—each chick
is equipped with a coat
that is fluffy and thick.

As the days turn to weeks
since their mothers' goodbye,
"Will she ever come back?"
all the little chicks cry.

The sea-ice is shifting . . .
oh no—are they drifting?
Then a swell of emotion
erupts from the ocean!

As thousands of penguins
begin to arrive
squawking, *"Mama is coming!"*
"I'm back—I'm alive!"

But how will each mother
find each little baby?
In thousands of penguins—
Impossible?
Maybe . . .

For emperor penguins
can all make a sound
that's completely unique.
So each baby is found!

After months on the ice
and a very long fast,
the papa hands over
to Mama-at last!

*"I kept our egg safe
with the help of my feet,
and now it's MY turn
to find something to eat!"*

All about the EMPEROR PENGUIN

Emperor penguins are the largest penguin species, standing around four feet when fully grown. They live in Antarctica on great sheets of sea ice, and dive deep in the icy ocean to hunt for food.

Between May and June, the female lays a single egg and carefully passes it over to the top of her partner's feet. Then she leaves to find food, while her mate stays behind to care for their egg.

This he does for an incredible nine weeks, sometimes more, keeping the egg above the freezing ground on his feet, covered by a flap of skin called a brood pouch.

As soon as the females return—plump and well fed—they find their partner by using a unique call. Once reunited, they regurgitate food into their chick's hungry mouth. And finally, the papa penguins head off to find something to eat!

After around 65 days of incubation, the eggs hatch and the fluffy penguin chicks emerge.

Colonies of hundreds—or thousands—of males huddle together for warmth. To keep things fair, they slowly rotate, shuffling around to take turns being in the warmer center.

In temperate waters
not far from the shore,
a shy little creature is
roaming the floor . . .

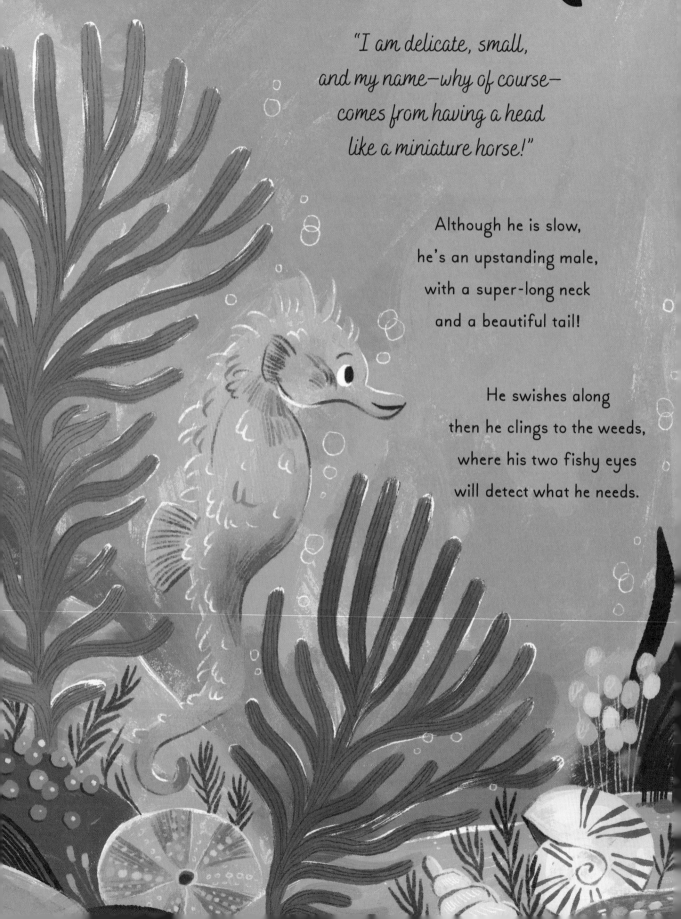

The DANCE of the SEAHORSES

"I am delicate, small,
and my name—why of course—
comes from having a head
like a miniature horse!"

Although he is slow,
he's an upstanding male,
with a super-long neck
and a beautiful tail!

He swishes along
then he clings to the weeds,
where his two fishy eyes
will detect what he needs.

He says,
"All bony and spiny, I'm ever-so tiny,
I wait for the love of my life.
A nozzle-nosed prancer,
a wonderful dancer . . .
she's all that I want from a wife!"

She says,
"All bony and spiny, I'm ever-so tiny,
I ramble and bob through the sea.
I don't want a chancer—no!
Only a dancer,
to do all his dancing for me!"

"Yippee!" he declares.
"Right on time—never late!"
As their two tails entwine,
"Shall we go on a . . . date?"

And twirling together
they shimmy and prance
for the rest of the day
in a wonderful dance . . .

From the tips of their tails
to the nibs of their noses,
the seahorses sway,
striking several poses . . .

They spin and encircle,
their two tummies touch,
then she says, "Take my eggs—
for I love you so much . . ."

The male has a ready-made
pouch for their brood.
It is here he will keep them
and give them their food.

Off she slips through the sea
with a bob and a swish
to go hunting herself
for crustaceans and fish.

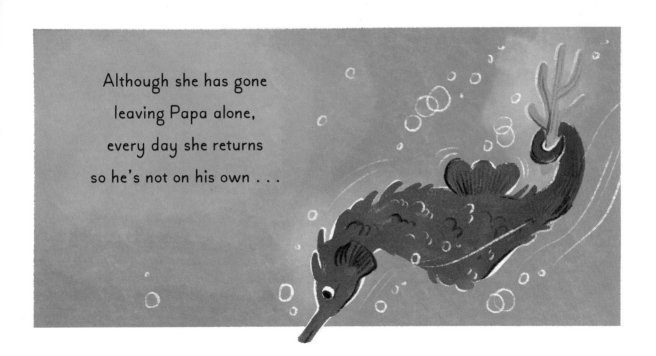

Although she has gone
leaving Papa alone,
every day she returns
so he's not on his own . . .

"*Good morning!*" she bobs,
and the little fish kiss,
then continue their dancing
in marital bliss.

"How are the babies?"
she asks. "Are they fine?"
And her partner replies,
"They are simply divine!"

While their parents embrace
as they dance to and fro,
safe and snug in his tummy
the sea-babies grow.

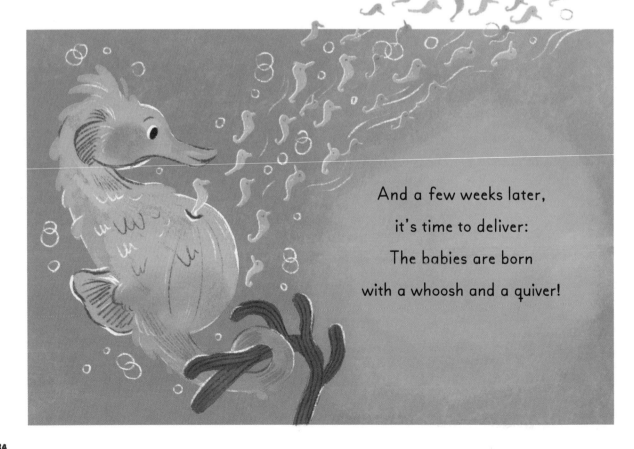

And a few weeks later,
it's time to deliver:
The babies are born
with a whoosh and a quiver!

Ever-so tiny, they flick
and they prance.
"Goodbye!" cry out their parents,
"Now on with the dance!"

All about THE SEAHORSE

Seahorses are shy, enchanting little fish, named after the fact that their heads looks like a horse's. They have long, bony bodies and swim upright, using the small pectoral fins on their heads to steer.

Seahorses pair up in a partnership that lasts for life. Their "dates" include is an intricate dance that can last for up to 8 hours.

There are around 40 species of seahorse. These tiny, spiny predators live in the calm, weedy shallows of warm, temperate seas.

Once a partnership has been established, the female seahorse transfers her eggs into her partner's pouch. This is specially designed to work like a womb, protecting, feeding, and removing any waste from the growing eggs.

Then the female leaves to feed on shrimp and fish eggs. Each day, she returns to her partner and together they dance around their ocean home together.

After about 2-4 weeks, the seahorse daddy is ready to give birth. Strong contractions spray showers of baby seahorses into the water. These minscule "fry" cling together as they are carried away by the current.

Their parents continue to dance together every day in a tender, delicate seahorse ballet, and soon many more babies will be on the way!

The moon rises high,
gleaming silver and ghostly.
The beach is deserted
and quiet—well, mostly . . .

The SALTY TEARS of the SEA TURTLE

A sky full of stars
lights the yellow-white land
while the heat of the night
warms a beach full of sand.

And something is happening
under the ground—
tiny voices are calling
without any sound . . .

Soon there's a scooping,
a digging and scratching . . .
The sand is expanding
and something is hatching!

Flotillas of miniature
turtles emerge
and immediately move
to the sea in a surge.

They shuffle and scrape,
in a scuffle they hurtle—
a moving and magical
carpet of turtle!

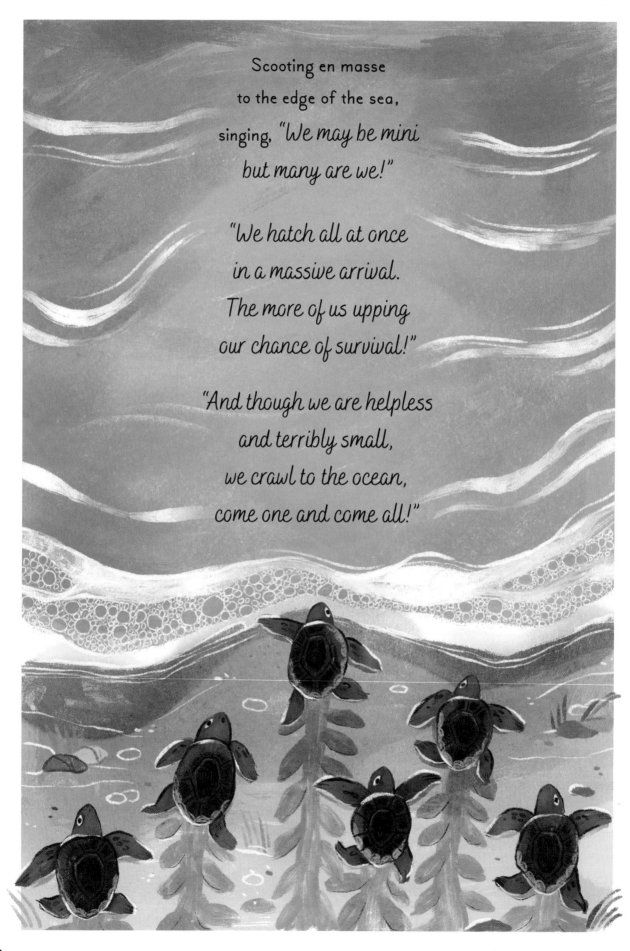

Scooting en masse
to the edge of the sea,
singing, "We may be mini
but many are we!"

"We hatch all at once
in a massive arrival.
The more of us upping
our chance of survival!"

"And though we are helpless
and terribly small,
we crawl to the ocean,
come one and come all!"

Into the water, now
bobbing and floating
with flippers a-flapping
as if they are boating.

Their life has begun with goodbyes,
and now friendless,
the turtles set off on
a journey that's endless.

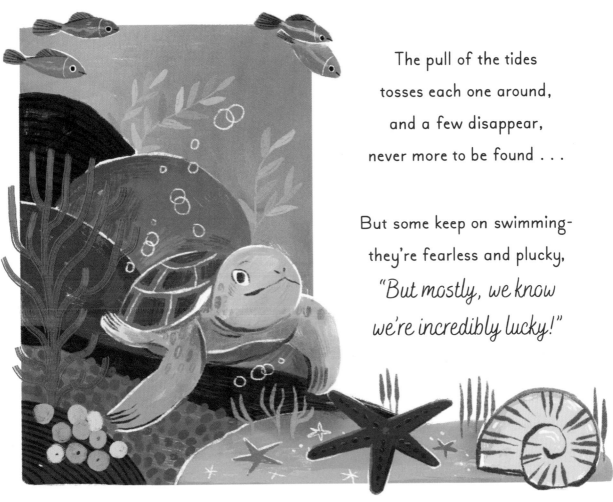

The pull of the tides
tosses each one around,
and a few disappear,
never more to be found . . .

But some keep on swimming-
they're fearless and plucky,
*"But mostly, we know
we're incredibly lucky!"*

"We swim through the ocean
to find what we seek,
while our shells grow enormous
along with our beaks!"

As the days turn to weeks
and the weeks become years,
every turtle, each one,
sheds an ocean of tears.

"Don't worry," they say,
"We're not sad like you think.
We are just shedding the salt
from the water we drink!"

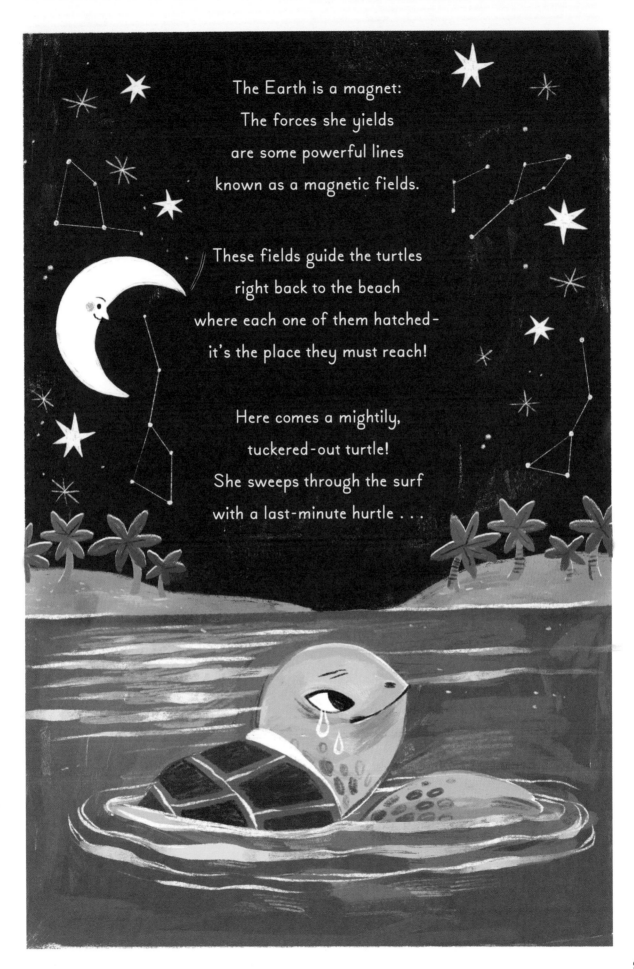

The Earth is a magnet:
The forces she yields
are some powerful lines
known as a magnetic fields.

These fields guide the turtles
right back to the beach
where each one of them hatched–
it's the place they must reach!

Here comes a mightily,
tuckered-out turtle!
She sweeps through the surf
with a last-minute hurtle . . .

She crawls up the beach
and she finds a good patch,
knowing this is the place
where her babies will hatch . . .

Her eggs safely buried,
she crosses the shore
and returns to the ocean
to journey once more.

*"My internal compass
is feeling the force.
I need to keep swimming
and swimming, of course!"*

The moon rises up
looking pallid and ghostly,
the beach is deserted
and quiet-well, mostly . . .

All about the GREEN SEA TURTLE

The green sea turtle gets its name from the green fat found beneath its shell. Turtle tears come not from sadness, but salt excretion glands in the corners of their eyes, which "cry" tears to get rid of the excess salt in their bodies.

1. The baby turtles hatch and emerge from the nest to find the bright horizon.

2. As soon as they've set eyes on the light of the ocean, the hatchlings set out to sea.

Green turtles have an excellent internal compass but can still get lost or confused by artificial lights or noises.

5. Female turtles carve out an egg chamber about 30 inches deep in the sand, where they lay their eggs. The eggs incubate for 49-62 days before hatching.

3. Once they reach maturity, females will return to the beach where they were born.

4. Each beach has its own unique magnetic pattern and this pattern is imprinted in the turtle's brain. So they navigate their way home, guided by Earth's magnetic fields.

So many stories—still time for one more . . .
Can you see all those seashells upon
the sea floor?

The HERMIT CRAB'S NEW HOME

Down by the beach
on the soft grainy sand,
some hermit crabs live
in a fine crabby band . . .

These snappy crustaceans
are famous for giving.
They live in a group
and they share for a living!

Community-minded
and one of a kind,
every hermit will forage
and use what they find!

But one sunny morning
the smallest one cries,
"From the tip of my tail
to my two beady eyes . . ."

"My body is changing—
it's getting so shabby.
I don't mean to moan
but I feel kind of . . . crabby!"

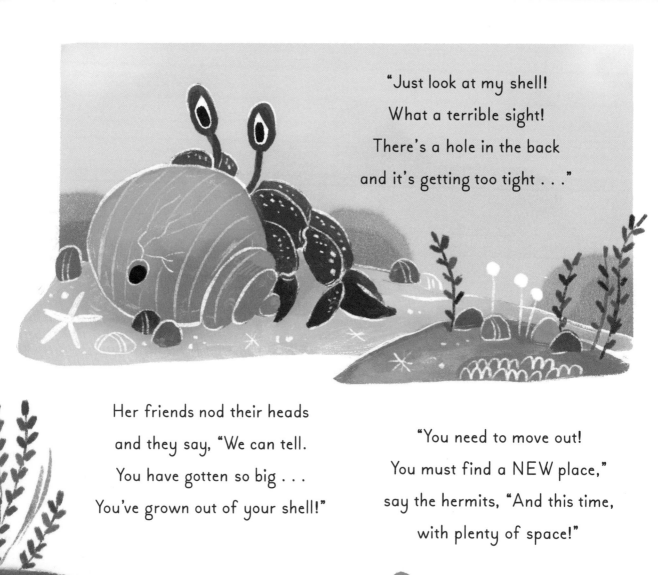

"Just look at my shell!
What a terrible sight!
There's a hole in the back
and it's getting too tight . . ."

Her friends nod their heads
and they say, "We can tell.
You have gotten so big . . .
You've grown out of your shell!"

"You need to move out!
You must find a NEW place,"
say the hermits, "And this time,
with plenty of space!"

The crab runs away
on her scurrying feet,
singing, "I need a new shell
to make me complete!"

And look! There's a whopper
washed up in the foam,
"It's lovely and roomy –
could this be my home?"

She measures the shell –
but it's not the right size.
"I'll have to keep searching,"
she says, then:

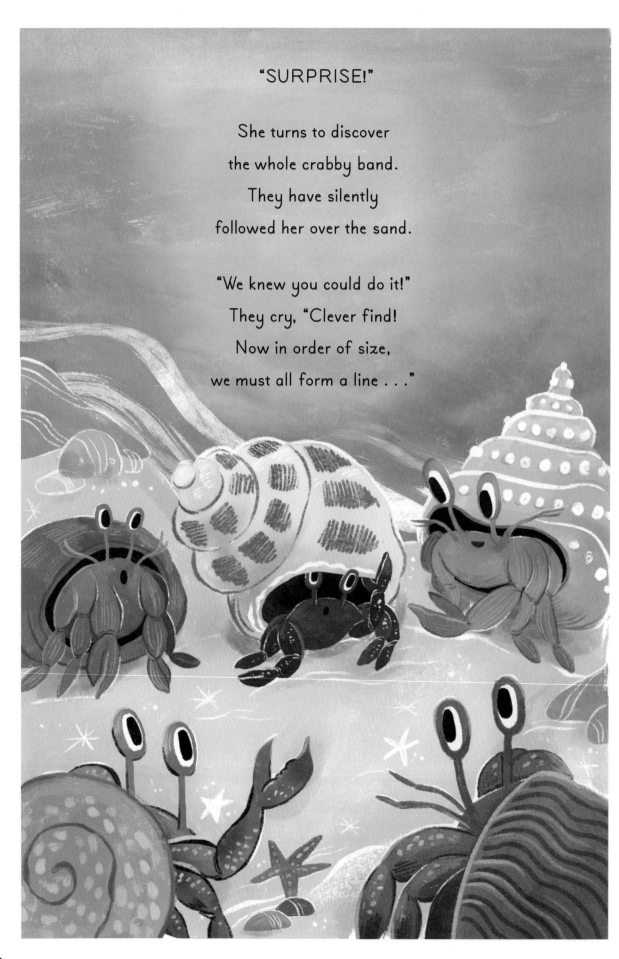

"SURPRISE!"

She turns to discover
the whole crabby band.
They have silently
followed her over the sand.

"We knew you could do it!"
They cry, "Clever find!
Now in order of size,
we must all form a line . . ."

After a shuffle,
the biggest goes first,
and the littlest hermit
is last. "That's the worst!"

But see what is happening?
Biggest to small,
they are all swapping shells,
meaning new shells for all!

Each crab is delighted
and clapping their claws.
Every hermit unites
in a round of applause!

These snappy crustaceans
are famous for giving.
They beachcomb for homes
and they share for a living!

The hermit is happy,
her heart full of love.
"See? My new shell is perfect—
it fits like a glove!"

"And so I'll keep growing
until I am done.
Then I'll go find another—
'cuz sharing is fun!"

All about the HERMIT CRAB

Hermit crabs have a name that makes them sound like solitary creatures, but they're not. In fact, they are extremely sociable, often living in communities of hundreds.

Hermits have a hard exoskeleton but their tail is soft and needs protection.

They find shelter in the form of another sea creature's discarded shell. The crabs recycle these, finding larger and larger shells to move into as they grow.

The crabs are cooperative. When a new shell is found, a small group will gather around and form a line in order of size. The biggest crab tries on the new shell first and if it fits, their old shell is up for grabs!

Resourceful, recycling, sociable, and cooperative hermit crabs live about 30-40 years or more, depending on the species.

Astonishing creatures
and curious fish,
every one is a wonder
with only one wish . . .

From corals to crevices,
each fin and shell
has a wonderful
5-minute story to tell!

FURTHER READING

Oceanarium: Welcome to the Museum by Loveday Trinick and illustrated by Teagan White

The Big Book of Blue by Yuval Zommer

Earth's Aquarium: Discover 15 Real-life Water Worlds by Alexander Kaufman and illustrated by Mariana Rodrigues

Explore every bit of this book with a wondrous eye!
– Mona K

Inspired by the work of conservationists and photographers Paul Nicklen and Christina Mittermeier, and the charity Sea Change Project.
– Gabby D

The illustrations in this book were created using gouache, colored pencil, and digital media.
Set in Bakerie, Claytonia, Pistachio, and Quicksand.

Library of Congress Control Number 2024939297
ISBN 978-1-4197-7693-9

Text © 2024 Gabby Dawnay
Illustrations © 2024 Mona K
Book design by Nicola Price and Maisy Ruffels

Printed and bound in China
10 9 8 7 6 5 4 3 2 1

ABRAMS The Art of Books
195 Broadway, New York, NY 10007
abramsbooks.com